PYTHON
PROGRAMMING:

A STEP BY STEP GUIDE FROM BEGINNER TO ADVANCE

Leonard Eddison

© Copyright 2018 by Leonard Eddison
All rights reserved.

This document is geared towards providing exact and reliable information with regards to the topic and issue covered. The publication is sold with the idea that the publisher is not required to render accounting, officially permitted, or otherwise, qualified services. If advice is necessary, legal or professional, a practiced individual in the profession should be ordered.

- From a Declaration of Principles which was accepted and approved equally by a Committee of the American Bar Association and a Committee of Publishers and Associations.

In no way is it legal to reproduce, duplicate, or transmit any part of this document in either electronic means or in printed format. Recording of this publication is strictly prohibited and any storage of this document is not allowed unless with written permission from the publisher. All rights reserved.

The information provided herein is stated to be truthful and consistent, in that any liability, in terms of inattention or otherwise, by any usage or abuse of any policies, processes, or directions contained within is the solitary and utter responsibility of the recipient reader. Under no circumstances will any legal responsibility or blame be held against the publisher for any reparation, damages, or monetary loss due to the information herein, either directly or indirectly.

Respective authors own all copyrights not held by the publisher.

The information herein is offered for informational purposes solely and is universal as so. The presentation of the information is without contract or any type of guarantee assurance.

The trademarks that are used are without any consent, and the publication of the trademark is without permission or backing by the trademark owner. All trademarks and brands within this book are for clarifying purposes only and are the owned by the owners themselves, not affiliated with this document.

Table of contents

PYTHON PROGRAMMING: 1

A STEP BY STEP GUIDE FROM BEGINNER TO ADVANCE 1

Introduction 7

CHAPTER ONE: I WANT TO START PROGRAMMING 10

CHAPTER TWO: WHY LEARN PYTHON. 13

TOP 5 REASONS 13

CHAPTER THREE: PROS AND CONS OF LEANING PYTHON...17

CHAPTER FOUR: HOW TO INSTALL PYTHON 27

CHAPTER FIVE: INTERPRETER, INTERACTIVE 32

CHAPTER SIX: PYTHON or PERL 34

CHAPTER SEVEN: OBJECT ORIENTED 45

CHAPTER EIGHT: MODULES....................................48

CHAPTER NINE: LET'S DIVE IN 52

CHAPTER TEN: VARIOUS TYPES OF DATA 56

CHAPTER ELEVEN: SYNTAX......................................81

CHAPTER TWELVE: FUNCTIONS 93

CHAPTER THIRTEEN: CLASSES...............................108

CHAPTER FOURTEEN: WHAT CAUSES FATAL ERRORS AND HOW TO FIX IT 111

CHAPTER FIFTHEEN: BEST PRACTICES FOR HANDLING WEBSITE ERRORS..114

CHAPTER SIXTEEN: WHY PYTHON IS HERE TO STAY 123

CONCLUSION 131

Page Intentionally Left Blank

Introduction

Chances are, if you're viewing this page, you're new to Python.

You might even be new to Programming altogether. Either way, you have come to the right place and chosen the right language!

Python is an easy to learn programming language, and I hope this book will convince you to take in consideration using it for your future projects. It is a great language for either beginners who are approaching the programming world or if you are already a professional programmer.

You don't have to be an expert to comprehend this book due to the fact that it will explain Python and the basic programming functions through a simple step-by-step process. It is also appropriate for those who are approaching computer programming for the first time.

You don't need to have a particular OS in order to run Python because it works perfectly on every OS.

In the first chapters, we will discuss the importance of learning how to use Python, its pros and cons.

In the fourth chapter, we will go through the process to install Python on Windows, Mac, and Linux.

From the fifth chapter, we will start a step-by-step process designed to take you from a pure beginner, who is approaching the programming world, to a student ready to start more complex projects.

I hope you enjoy this book...

Page intentionally left blank

CHAPTER ONE: I WANT TO START PROGRAMMING

Python is a powerful, high-level, object-oriented programming language created by Guido van Rossum.

It has simple, easy-to-use syntax, making it the perfect language for someone who is trying to learn computer programming for the first time.

This is a comprehensive guide on how to get started in Python, why you should learn it, and how you can learn it.

What is Python? - The Basics

Before getting started, let's get familiarized with the language.

Python is a general-purpose language. It has a wide range of applications from Web development (like: Django and Bottle), scientific and mathematical computing (Orange, SymPy, NumPy) to desktop graphical user Interfaces (Pygame, Panda3D).

The syntax of the language is clean, and the length of the code is relatively short. It's fun to work in Python because it allows you to think about the problem rather than focus on the syntax.

<u>3 Reasons to Choose Python as First Language</u>

-Simple Elegant Syntax

Programming in Python is fun. It's easier to understand and write Python code. Why? The syntax feels natural. Take this source code for example:

```
a = 2
b = 3
Sum = a + b
Print (sum)
```

Even if you have never programmed before, you can easily guess that this program adds two numbers and prints it.

Not overly strict

You don't need to define the type of variable in Python. Also, it's not necessary to add a semicolon at the end of the statement.

Python enforces you to follow good practices (like proper indentation). These small things can make learning much easier for beginners.

Great community and Support

Python has a large supporting community. There are numerous active forums online, which can be handy if you are stuck.

CHAPTER TWO: WHY LEARN PYTHON.

TOP 5 REASONS

Python is one of the most robust and dynamic programming languages being used today. It stresses code readability, and because of its syntax as well as implementation, programmers have to write fewer codes in comparison to Java and C++. Memory management in Python is done automatically, and several standard libraries are available for the programmer. After completing a certification course in Python training, a programmer can gain experience in various top IT companies.

Python programming supports numerous styles, such as functional programming, imperative, and object-oriented styles.

Here are the top five reasons a computer programmer must learn the Python language:

<u>Ease of learning</u>- Python has been created with the newcomer in mind. Completion of basic tasks requires less code in Python compared to other languages. The codes are usually 3-5 times shorter than Java and 5-10 times smaller than C++. Python codes are easily readable, and with a little knowledge, new developers can learn a lot just by looking at the code.

<u>Highly preferred for web development- Python</u> consists of an array of frameworks that are useful in designing a website. Among these frameworks, Django is the most popular one for Python development. Due to these frameworks, web designing with Python has immense flexibility. The number of websites online today is close to 1 billion, and with the ever-increasing scope, it is natural that Python programming will continue to be an important skill for web developers.

<u>Considered ideal for start-ups-</u> Time and budget are vital constraints for any new product or service in a company and more so if it is a startup. One can create a product that differentiates itself from the rest in any language. However, for quick development, less code and lower cost, Python is the ideal language. Python can easily scale up any complex application and can be handled by a small team. Not only can you save resources, but you also get to develop applications in the right direction with Python.

<u>Unlimited availability of resources and testing framework</u>- Several resources for Python are available today, and these are constantly being updated. As a result, it is rare that a Python developer gets stuck. The vast standard library provides inbuilt functionalities. Its built-in testing framework enables speedy workflows and less debugging time.

<u>Fat paycheques-</u> Today, top IT companies, such as Google, Yahoo, IBM, and Nokia, make use of Python. Among all programming languages, it has had amazing growth over the last few years.

CHAPTER THREE: PROS AND CONS OF LEANING PYTHON

Python is a high-level, interpreted, and general-purpose dynamic programming language that focuses on code readability. The syntax in Python helps the programmers code in fewer steps compared to Java or C++.

Python is widely used in big companies because of its multiple programming paradigms. They usually involve imperative and object-oriented functional programs. It has a comprehensive and large standard library that has automatic memory management and dynamic features.

Why Companies Prefer Python?

Python has topped the charts in recent years over other programming languages like C, C++, and Java and is widely used by programmers. The language has undergone a drastic change since its release 25 years ago as many add-on features are introduced. The Python 1.0 had the module system of Modula-3 and interacted with Amoeba Operating System with varied functioning tools. Python 2.0, introduced in the year 2000, had the features of garbage collector and Unicode Support. Python 3.0, introduced in the year 2009, had a constructive design that avoids duplicate modules and constructs. With the added features, now companies are using Python 3.5.

Software development companies prefer the Python language because of its versatile features and fewer programming codes. Nearly 14% of programmers use it on operating systems like UNIX, Linux, Windows, and Mac OS. The programmers in big companies use Python as it has created a mark for itself in software development with characteristic features like-

- Interactive
- Interpreted
- Modular
- Dynamic
- Object-oriented
- Portable

- High level
- Extensible in C++ & C

- <u>Advantages or Benefits of Python</u>

The Python language has multiple applications in software development companies, such as in gaming, web frameworks and applications, language development, prototyping, graphic design applications etc. This provides the language with a higher plethora of advantages than other programming languages used in the industry. Some of its advantages are:

- Extensive Support Libraries

It provides a large standard library that includes areas like string operations, Internet, web service tools, operating system interfaces, and protocols. Most of the highly used programming tasks are already scripted into it, which limits the length of codes you need to write in Python.

- Integration Feature

Python integrates the Enterprise Application, making it easy to develop Web services by invoking COM or COBRA components. It has powerful control capabilities as it calls directly through C, C++, or Java via Jython. Python also processes XML and other markup languages as it can run on all modern operating systems through the same byte code.

- Improved Programmer's Productivity

The language has extensive support libraries and clean object-oriented designs that increase programmers' productivity by two to ten fold while using languages like Java, VB, Perl, C, C++ and C#.

- Productivity

Its strong process integration features, unit testing framework, and enhanced control capabilities contribute to the increased speed for most applications and productivity. It is a great option to build a scalable multi-protocol network application.

Limitations or Disadvantages of Python

Python has varied advantageous features, and programmers prefer this language to other programming languages because it is easy to learn and code. However, this language has still not made its place in some computing areas, including Enterprise Development Shops. Therefore, this language may not solve some of the enterprise solutions, and some limitations are:

- **Difficulty Using Other Languages**

Python lovers become so accustomed to its features and its extensive libraries that they face problems when learning or working on other programming languages. Python experts may see the declaring of cast "values" or variable "types", syntactic requirements of adding curly braces or semi colons as an onerous task.

- **Weak in Mobile Computing**

Python has made its presence on many desktop and server platforms, but it is seen as a weak language for mobile computing. This is the reason few mobile applications, like Carbonnelle, are built in it.

- **Slow Speed**

Python runs with the help of an interpreter instead of the compiler, which causes it to slow down because of the compilation and the execution that helps it to work normally. On the other hand, it can be seen that it is fast for many web applications.

- **Run-time Errors**

The Python language is dynamically typed so it has many design restrictions reported by some Python developers. It is even seen that it requires more testing time, and the errors always show up when the applications are finally run.

- **Underdeveloped Database Access Layers**

As compared to popular technologies, like JDBC and ODBC, Python's database access layer is found to be a bit underdeveloped and primitive.

However, it cannot be applied in enterprises that need smooth interaction of complex legacy data.

PCAP: Programming Essentials in Python

Python is a general-purpose programming language used to build just about anything. Python is key for backend web development, data analysis, artificial intelligence, and scientific computing, all of which are key for pursuing IT careers. With PCAP: Programming Essentials in Python, you learn to design, write, debug, and run programs encoded in the Python language. No prior programming knowledge is required. The course begins with the very basics, guiding you step by step until you become adept at solving more complex problems. The course aligns to the PCAP – Python Certified Associate Programmer certification, validating your expertise to employers and expanding your IT and IoT career opportunities.

- Develop a working knowledge for how computers operate and how computer programs are executed.
- Evolve critical thinking and problem-solving skills using an algorithmic approach.
- Learn about the programmer's role in the software development process.
- Translate real-world issues into computer-solvable problems.
- Connect with the global Cisco Networking Academy community.

CHAPTER FOUR: HOW TO INSTALL PYTHON (Windows, Mac and Linux)

In order to install Python, first, we need to download the right version for our OS.

The process is well-explained on www.python.org (the official website), where we will find the most suitable version for us. For that reason, we will keep the process explanation as short as possible.

Windows

In order to install Python on Windows, you first have to check the official site and click the voice download that you will find on the main menu.

At that point, you will see a page from which you can download your desired version of Python.

The process to download and install the program is very well-explained and straightforward.

From the moment the download is complete, we can start to write our first code:

Let's try with the simplest directive you can write: the "print" directive.

With this particular directive, the program will simply print out a line.

For this example, we will use the words "Let's start"

The code will appear like this:

print("Let's start")

Let's start

Linux

Chances are, if you own a computer that uses Linux, you will find python already installed. To verify it, just try to look for "Python" between your programs.

If you don't already have Python installed, you can download Python starting from the source code.

We'll get into that later.

Mac OS X

It's likely that you already have Python installed on this OS. Again, to verify it, you can look for the word "Python" in your Mac.

If you can't find Python on your device, you can easily download it from the site, using the .dmg format (disk image).

Source code

We need to choose our desired version of the program from the website before beginning to complete the source code.

Once you find the paragraph "All others", you will obtain the link that recalls the Source code for your version (example: Python - 3.0 . tgz.).

After we download the file, we need to extract the files in it. The tgz. format should be well-known to Linux and Mac users.

Searching on Google for the tgz and windows strings, we can get the utility to extract the format.

Once you do that, you should be able to run Python like any other program.

CHAPTER FIVE: INTERPRETER, INTERACTIVE

For most programming languages, you need to write the source code, compiling, and sometimes link the libraries in order to run the program.

With Python, everything is easier due to the fact that it allows you to run the source code directly (that is why it is defined as **Interpreter**) or even to write the instructions straight from its command prompt without creating or editing a source file (**Interactive).**

Sure, this last feature could seem a little odd, but we will see that, starting from the bottom, to try some new features or to test small parts from the your program, this feature is extremely fast and useful.

With the Interactive mode, you can easily play around and experiment with new syntax variations.

CHAPTER SIX: PYTHON or PERL

Both Python and Perl are mature, open source, general purpose, high level, and interpreted programming languages. But the usage statistics posted on various websites depict that Python is currently more popular than Perl. Hence, a software developer can enhance his career prospects by switching from Perl to Python.

A beginner can further learn and use the Python programming language without putting extra time and effort. However, you must not switch to a new programming language just because of its popularity and usage. You must keep in mind the major differences between the two programming languages while deciding about migrating from Perl to Python.

12 Points You Must Keep in Mind while Switching from Perl to Python

1) Design Goal

Perl was originally designed as a scripting language to simplify report processing capabilities. It comes with built-in text processing capability. On the other hand, Python was designed initially as a hobby programming language. But it was designed with features to help programmers build applications with concise, readable, and reusable code. The two programming languages still differ in the categories of features and performance.

2) Syntax Rules

The syntax rules of both Python and Perl are influenced by several other programming languages. For instance, Perl borrows features from a number of programming languages, including C, shell script, sed,

AWK, and Lisp. Likewise, Python implements functional programming features in a manner similar to Lisp. In addition to being easy to use, the Python syntax rules further enable programmers to except many concepts with less and readable code.

3) Family of Languages

Perl belongs to a family of high-level programming languages that includes Perl 5 and Perl 6. The versions 5 and 6 of Perl are compatible with each other. A developer can easily migrate from Perl 5 to Perl 6 without putting extra time and effort. The different versions of Python are not compatible with each other. Hence, a programmer has to choose from two distinct versions of the programming language.

4) Ways to Achieve Same Results

Python enables programmers to express concepts without writing long lines of code. But it requires programmers to accomplish tasks or achieve results in a specific and single way. On the other hand, Perl enables programmers to accomplish a single task or achieve the same results in a number of ways. Hence, many programmers find Perl to be more flexible than Python, but the multiple ways to achieve the same result often make the code written in Perl messy and the application difficult to maintain.

5) Web Scripting Language

Perl was originally designed as a UNIX scripting language. Many developers use Perl as a scripting language to avail its built-in text processing capabilities. However, there are many web developers who complain that Perl is slower than other widely used scripting languages. Python is also used widely by programmers for web application development. But it lacks built-in web development capabilities. Hence, developers have to avail various frameworks and tools to write web applications in Python efficiently and rapidly.

6) Web Application Frameworks

Most developers nowadays avail the tools and features provided by various frameworks to build web applications efficiently and rapidly. Perl web programmers have options to choose from an array of frameworks, including Catalyst, Dancer, Mojolicious, Poet, Interchange, Jifty, and Gantry. Likewise, the web developers have the option to use a number of Python web frameworks, including Django, Flask, Pyramid, Bottle, and Cherrypy. However, the number of Python web frameworks is much higher than the number of Perl web frameworks.

7) Usage

As mentioned earlier, both Python and Perl are general-purpose programming languages. Hence, each programming language is used to develop a variety of software applications. Perl is used widely for graphic and network programming, system administration, and development of finance and biometric applications, whereas Python comes with a robust standard library that simplifies web application development, scientific computing, big data solution development, and artificial intelligence tasks. Hence, developers prefer using Python for development of advanced and mission-critical software applications.

8) Performance and Speed

A number of studies have shown that Python is slower than other programming languages, like Java and C++. Developers frequently explore ways to enhance the execution speed of Python code.

Someone even replaced default Python runtime with their own custom runtime to make the Python applications run faster. Many programmers find Perl to be faster than Python. Many web developers use Perl as a scripting language to make web applications faster and deliver enhanced user experience.

9) Structured Data Analysis

At the moment, big data is one of the hottest trends in software development. Many enterprises nowadays build custom applications for collecting, storing, and analyzing a huge amount of structured and unstructured data. The PDL provided by Perl enables developers to analyze big data. The built-in text processing capability of Perl further simplifies and speeds up analysis of a huge amount of structured data. But Python is used widely by programmers for data analysis. The developers further take advantage of robust Python libraries, like

Numpy, to process and analyze huge volumes of data in a faster and more efficient way.

10) JVM Interoperability

At the moment, Java is one of the programming languages used widely for development of desktop, web, and mobile applications. In comparison to Perl, Python interoperates with Java Virtual Machine (JVM) seamlessly and efficiently. Hence, the developers have the option to write Python code that runs smoothly on JVM, while taking advantage of robust Java APIs and objects. The interoperability helps programmers to build application by targeting the popular Java platform while writing code in Python instead of Java.

11) Advanced Object Oriented Programming

Both Perl and Python are object-oriented programming languages. But Python implements advanced object oriented programming languages in a better way than Perl. While writing code in Perl, programmers still need to use packages instead of classes. Many developers find it difficult to keep the code simple and readable while writing object oriented code in Perl. But Perl makes it easier for programmers to accomplish a variety of tasks simply by using one liners on the command line.

12) Text Processing Capability

Unlike Python, Perl was designed with built-in text processing capabilities. Hence, many programmers prefer using Perl for report generation. Perl further makes it easier for programmers to perform regex and string comparison operations, like matching, replacement, and substitution. It does not require developers to write additional code to perform exception handling and I/O operations. Hence, many programmers prefer Perl to Python when they have to build applications to process textual data or generate reports.

CHAPTER SEVEN: OBJECT ORIENTED

We won't get into this expression in detail, (a universally accepted definition still doesn't exist). What we can say about this paradigm is that it means to think about the problem solution, not as a succession of instructions, but as objects and its respective attributes.

Python programmers can write high quality and modular code by using classes and objects.

With an object oriented language, we can face the problem with a different approach. For instance, we can define an object, give it a name, and from that moment, we can forget the definition due to the fact that it has been already saved.

Furthermore, we can save the physical state inside the file in order to open it only once. By doing so, our object will give us all the reading and writing functions we need.

<u>Let's take an example of Class</u>

>>> class fruit:

"""   tipo = "vegetable"

"""

```
>>> apple = fruit ()
>>> print apple.tipo
Vegetable
>>>
```

CHAPTER EIGHT: MODULES

In order to use a programming language, you often need to import several libraries that you will need in order to find codes.

A Python users' life is simplified due to the fact that you can find a ton of tested and functioning libraries.

Libraries in Python are called "modules".

"Modules" are pre-written Python codes that you "import" in your Python program. Since there are many tasks that people commonly do, we have modules that people have written that do these tasks for you, and they usually do them in the cleanest and most efficient way possible. Sometimes, you will see people refer to "DRY." This stands for Don't Repeat Yourself, which often also translates into "Don't Repeat Someone Else."

The phrase "wrapper" means that someone has placed, like a wrapper, Python code over another language. So, when you have a Python wrapper around a C++ code, what someone has done is written some Python code that interacts with the C++ language. This allows you to make use of various aspects of the language being wrapped, in this case C++, without actually needing to know or understand that language.

Thus, Python can be used to make games, do data analysis, control robot and hardware, create GUIs, or even to create websites.

"GUI" stands for Graphical User Interface and is used to describe a program that incorporates graphics to make the program more interactive for the user.

Now, let's see how to import a library on Python.

You can gain access to a module by simply using the "import" statement. Doing this, you will execute the code of the module.

In order to have access to a module, the user must first look for a built-in module in Python (Python has a wide variety of build-in functions that allow the user to start its journey in programming; if the user wants to experiment with different functions, he/she may need to import a module). If the corresponding module is not already built in, we need to import it.

Let's see a practical example:

Let's say that I want to import a module called "example1".

I'll run the statement for that module:

Import example1

And it's as easy as that.

CHAPTER NINE: LET'S DIVE IN

Now, we will dive into Python, discovering the various commands, lists, strings, and so on…

IDLE

You will find "IDLE" (Integrated Development Environment) in the main menu, and it will allow you to edit, run, and test the codes that you will create.

IDLE has the following features:

coded in Python, using the tkinter GUI toolkit

cross-platform: It has the same features whether you're using Windows, Unix, Mac OS X, or Linux

Python shell window (interactive interpreter) with colorizing of code input, output, and error messages

multi-window text editor with multiple undo, Python colorizing, smart indent, call tips, auto completion, and other features

search within any window, replace within editor windows, and search through multiple files (grep) debugger with persistent breakpoints, stepping, and viewing of global and local namespaces

configuration, browsers, and other dialogs

IDLE has two main window types: The first one is the Shell window, and the second is the Editor window. You can easily run multiple editor windows at the same time. Output windows are a subtype of edit window. They currently have the same top menu as the Editor windows but a different default title and context menu.

IDLE's menus change dynamically based on which window is currently selected.

Each menu documented below indicates which window type it is associated with.

Now, let's run IDLE and digit the command we already tried.

print("Let's start")

We can see how the program processes our command.

Since we don't want to digit the codes every time, we will now save the source code.

EDITING

Let's run the command File/New window that we will find in the IDLE menu, and we will open a new window without the command prompt.

In this new window, we will write our beloved code once again:

print("Let's start")

But this time, we click on the "file/save", and we save our file, naming it start.py in a directory.

Now, we can run our newly created program from IDLE with the command "run".

There are a lot of editors available to write Python programs. Let's see the most famous:

• Eclipse with PyDev: Eclipse has a massive community of developers, and it allows you a great level of customization.

- Eric: Eric writes in Python using qt framework, and it utilizes Scintilla, which is a source code editing component.
- PyCharm: It has its own free community, which is definitely useful when you're learning to code.
- Other good options may be: PyScripter, LeoEditor, Bluefish, Ptk, Spyder, and Geany.

CHAPTER TEN: VARIOUS TYPES OF DATA

Luckily for us, Python has a good set of built-in functions that perform very well especially for beginners.

We will now learn the main built-in function:

1. **The type function**: It returns the datatype of any arbitrary object. The type function can even take a variable and return it as datatype. You can use this function to compare different types of objects.

Let's see an example:

n=1

type(n)

<type 'int'>

    S=start

<type 'str'>

    import smtplib

    type (smtplib)

<type 'module'>

2. **The dir Command**: The syntax of dir in the following: dir([object]), dir allows us to obtain a list of valid attributes for a given object.

Let's see a practical example of how dir works:

```
class Person:
    def __dir__(self):
        return ['age', 'gender', 'salary']


carpenter = Person()
print(dir(carpenter))
```

This command will appear like this once you run it:

['age', 'gender', 'salary']

3. **List**: (Syntax: list([iterable])) this command has the purpose of creating a list whose items are the same and in the same order as *iterable*'s items; *iterable* may be

either a sequence, a container that supports iteration, or an iterator object.

Let's now see a simple list:

```
list = [2, 6 , 12]
list
```

Let's run the command, and the result will be the following:

2, 6, 12

In order to use values in lists, we can use the square brackets. Hhere's an example:

```
list1 = ['math', 'history', 1993, 1994];
list2 = [1, 2, 3, 4, 5, 6, 7 ];
print "list1[0]: ", list1[0]
print "list2[1:5]: ", list2[1:5]
```

Once we run it, we will have the following output:

list1[0]: math

list2[1:5]: [2, 3, 4, 5]

lists can be updated using the command append()

I'll give you an example:

list = ['math', 'history', 1993, 1994];

print "Value available at index 2 : "

print list[2]

list[2] = 1995;

print "New value available at index 2 : "

print list[2]

And the output will be the following:

Value available at index 2 :

1993

New value available at index 2 :

1995

We can also delete elements:

list1 = ['math', 'history', 1993, 1994];

```
print list1
del list1[2];
print "After deleting value at index 2 : "
print list1
```

With the following output:

['math', 'history', 1993, 1994]

After deleting value at index 2 :

['math', 'history', 1994]

There are some expressions that we can use with lists:

Length: len([1, 2, 3]) → 3

Concatenation: [1, 2, 3] + [4, 5, 6] → [1, 2, 3, 4, 5, 6]

Repetition: ['Let's start'] * 3 → ['Let's start', 'Let's start', 'Let's start']

Membership: 3 in [1, 2, 3] → True

In regard to list's built-in functions, I'll list the most important:

- cmp(list1, list2) → compares elements of both lists
- len(list) → gives the total length of the list
- max(list) → returns item from the list with max value
- min(list) → returns item from the list with min valuw
- list(seq) → converts a tuple into list (we'll see what a tuple is in a moment)

In regard to list's built-in methods, I'll list the most important:

- list.append(obj) → Appends object obj to list
- list.count(obj) → Returns count of how many times obj occurs in list
- list.extend(seq) → Appends the contents of seq to list
- list.index(obj) → Returns the lowest index in list that obj appears

- list.insert(index, obj) → Inserts object obj into list at offset index
- list.pop(obj=list[-1]) → Removes and returns last object or obj from list
- list.remove(obj) → Removes object obj from list
- list.reverse() → reverses objects of list in place
- list.sort([func]) → Sorts objects of list, use compare func if given

4. **Strings**: Strings in Python have a lot of interesting features. They are immutable (after you create a string, you cannot modify it), and if you need a new string, you can simply create it.

So, in the expression ('let's' + 'start'), we will have a new string composed of the two strings 'let's' and 'start'.

Let's see a practical example:

s = 'let's'

```
print s [1]           ## i
print len(s)          ##2
print s + ' start '   ## let's start
```

Now, let's see a couple of examples of strings using the *slicing* function.

```
s = "0123456789"
```

With the following function:

```
s [:5]
```

You can select the first 5 numbers

'01234'

With the following function:

```
s [-5:]
```

you can select the last 5 numbers

'56789'

Keep in mind that Python uses zero-based indexing; therefore, if str is 'hello' str[1] is 'e'.

In order to wrap, we need to utilize the backslash followed by "n". Let's see an example:

s = "8\n9\n10\nHi"

print s

8

9

10

HI

The "\n" character is a special one. Here is a list of the most important special characters:

1. "\t" is a tab
2. "\r" is a carriage return
3. "\\" is the literal backslash character.
4. "\b" is the backspace

We can use the "+" symbol to join two strings:

s = ex

p = ample

s + p

'example'

Or we can multiply a string using the "*" symbol:

s = example

s * 5

'exampleexampleexampleexampleexample'

In Python, we can find a lot of string methods (a method is similar to a function that runs on an object). We will now take a look at the most commonly used:

- s.lower(), s.upper() -- returns the lowercase or uppercase version of the string

- s.strip() -- returns a string with whitespace removed from the start and end

- s.isalpha()/s.isdigit()/s.isspace()... -- tests if all the string chars are in the various character classes

- s.startswith('other'), s.endswith('other') -- tests if the string starts or ends with the given other string

- s.find('other') -- searches for the given other string (not a regular expression) within s and returns the first index where it begins or -1 if not found

- s.replace('old', 'new') -- returns a string where all occurrences of 'old' have been replaced by 'new'

- s.split('delim') -- returns a list of substrings separated by the given delimiter. The delimiter is not a regular expression. It's just text.

- 'aaa,bbb,ccc'.split(',') -> ['aaa', 'bbb', 'ccc']. As a convenient special case s.split() (with no arguments) splits on all whitespace chars.

- s.join(list) -- opposite of split(), joins the elements in the given list using the string as the delimiter. e.g. '---'.join(['aaa', 'bbb', 'ccc']) -> aaa---bbb---ccc

5. Tuples

With the term "tuple", we are referring to a sequence of objects that are immutable in Python.

If a tuple is empty, it will appear as the following:

```
tup1 = ()
```

If a tuple includes even only one value, we have to include a comma:

```
tup1 = (1,)
```

Let's see some more tuples:

```
tup1 = ('dog', 'cat', 'fish', 'seal' )
tup2 = (1, 2, 3, 4 )
```

Tuples can be sliced, concatenated and more, just like strings, but in order to do that, we have to use square brackets:

```
tup1 = ('dog', 'cat', 'fish', 'seal')
tup2 = (1, 2, 3, 4 )
```

print "tup1[0]: ", tup1[0]

print "tup2[1:4]: ", tup2[2:3]

Once we execute this code, we will have this result:

tup1[0]: dog

tup2[1:4]: (3,)

If you were expecting a different output that is because tuples indices begin at 0.

As already said, tuples are immutable. If you need to add or delete elements, you have to create a new tuple. Let's see an example:

At first, we will look at how we can create a new tuple with the desired elements:

tup1 = (1, 2, 3)

tup2 = ('dog', 'cat', 'fish')

tup3 = tup1 + tup2

Now, we just have to run the print command, and this will be the result:

print (tup3)

(1, 2, 3, 'dog', 'cat', 'fish')

Lists and tuples are similar. The main difference is that, while lists can be modified at any time, tuples are immutable. Moreover, while tuples use parentheses, lists use square brackets.

Tuples, just like lists, respond to any general operation, like those we have seen in the chapter regarding lists (length, concatenation, repetition, membership and iteration).

We can find built-in functions also for tuples:

- cmp(tuple1, tuple2) → Compares elements of both tuples.
- len(tuple) → Gives the total length of the tuple.
- max(tuple) → Returns item from the tuple with max value.
- min(tuple) → Returns item from the tuple with

- min value tuple(seq) → Converts a list into tuple.

6. Sets

A set is a type of data that allows us to handle groups of elements. It creates a collection of unordered and unique elements. Set objects also support mathematical operations like union, intersection, difference, and symmetric difference.

Let's see an example:

a = set ('example')

b = set ('exile')

- a

{ 'e', 'x', 'a', 'm', 'p', 'l'}

As you can see, this set is missing the last "e", and that is because, as we said before, sets only contain unique elements.

But let's continue with our example:

- a – b (with this function, we can build a set formed only by the letters in a but not the letters in b)

{ 'a', 'm', 'p'}

- a | b (it takes the letters in a and in b)

{ 'e', 'x', 'a', 'm', 'p', 'l', 'i'}

- a & b (it takes the letters contained in both a and b)

{ 'e', 'x', 'l'}

- a ^ b (it takes the letters in a or in b but not in both)

{ 'a', 'm', 'p', 'l'}

Sets don't support indexing and slicing

In order to add elements, we will have to use the add() command for a single element and the update() command for multiple elements.

In order to remove elements, we will have to use discard() or remove(), whereas if we need to remove all the elements in the set, we can use clear().

Sets are useful to carry out mathematical operations. Let's see an example:

A = {1, 2, 3, 4, 5}

B = {4, 5, 6, 7, 8}

Now, there are 4 possible operations: union, intersection, difference, and symmetric difference. Let's see them in action:

1. Union: For this operation, we can use | operator or the method union()

initialize A and B

A = {1, 2, 3, 4, 5}

B = {4, 5, 6, 7, 8}

# use | operator
# Output: {1, 2, 3, 4, 5, 6, 7, 8}
print(A | B)

2. Intersection: This operation will include the elements that are common in both sets, and we will use the method intersection():

initialize A and B

A = {1, 2, 3, 4, 5}

B = {4, 5, 6, 7, 8}

use & operator

Output: {4, 5}

print(A & B)

3. Difference: With this operation, we can have the elements that appear in A but not in B or vice versa. It is performed using the method difference ():

initialize A and B

A = {1, 2, 3, 4, 5}

B = {4, 5, 6, 7, 8}

use - operator on A

Output: {1, 2, 3}

print(A – B)

4. Symmetric difference: This operation allows us to take the elements in both A and B, leaving aside those that appear in both. It is done through the method symmetric_difference():

initialize A and B

A = {1, 2, 3, 4, 5}

B = {4, 5, 6, 7, 8}

```
# use ^ operator
# Output: {1, 2, 3, 6, 7, 8}
print(A ^ B)
```

In Python, we can find a list of built-in methods for sets. I will list the most useful:

- add() → Add an element to a set
- clear() → Remove all elements from a set
- copy() → Return a shallow copy of a set
- difference() → Return the difference of two or more sets as a new set
- difference_update() → Remove all elements of another set from this set
- discard() → Remove an element from set if it is a member. (Do nothing if the element is not in set)
- intersection() → Return the intersection of two sets as a new set
- intersection_update() → Update the set with the intersection of itself and another

- isdisjoint() → Return True if two sets have a null intersection
- issubset() → Return True if another set contains this set
- issuperset() → Return True if this set contains another set
- pop() → Remove and return an arbitary set element. Raise KeyError if the set is empty
- remove() → Remove an element from a set. If the element is not a member, raise a KeyError
- symmetric_difference() → Return the symmetric difference of two sets as a new set
- symmetric_difference_update() → Update a set with the symmetric difference of itself and another
- union() → Return the union of sets in a new set
- update() → Update a set with the union of itself and others

- In Python, we can also find a list of built-in functions:
- all() Return True if all elements of the set are true (or if the set is empty).
- any() Return True if any element of the set is true. If the set is empty, return False.
- enumerate() Return an enumerate object. It contains the index and value of all the items of set as a pair.
- len() Return the length (the number of items) in the set. max() Return the largest item in the set.
- min() Return the smallest item in the set.
- sorted() Return a new sorted list from elements in the set(does not sort the set itself).
- sum() Retrun the sum of all elements in the set.

7.   dictionaries

Python has a built-in function, called the dictionary, which massively simplifies our work.

The dictionary is a set of keys, and we can extract the set of values given by it.

In order to build a dictionary, we can utilize the constructor dict(). Let's see it in action:

```
rooms = dict ()
rooms[ 'guest1' ] = '101'
rooms [ 'guest2' ] = '102'
```

The dictionary we just built will be like this:

Rooms

{ 'guest1' : '101' , 'guest2' : '102' }

We can easily extract and add new elements to our dictionary using the key method

Rooms.keys()

['guest1', 'guest2']

Other interesting functions are: has_key (useful to determine if an element is in the dictionary), del (useful to delete an element), clear, copy, fromkey, get, items, and so on...

Dictionaries in Python have many built-in methods. As usual, I'll list the most useful:

- clear() Remove all items from the dictionary.
- copy() Return a shallow copy of the dictionary.
- fromkeys(seq[, v]) Return a new dictionary with keys from seq and value equal to v (defaults to None).
- get(key[,d]) Return the value of key. If key does not exist, return d (defaults to None).
- items() Return a new view of the dictionary's items (key, value).
- keys() Return a new view of the dictionary's keys.
- pop(key[,d]) Remove the item with key and return its value or d if key is not found. If d is not provided and key is not found, raises KeyError.
- popitem() Remove and return an arbitary item (key, value). Raises KeyError if the dictionary is empty.

- setdefault(key[,d]) If key is in the dictionary, return its value. If not, insert key with a value of d and return d (defaults to None).
- update([other]) Update the dictionary with the key/value pairs from other, overwriting existing keys.
- values() Return a new view of the dictionary's values.

8. True, false and none

False and none are two constant objects in Python, referred to as Boolean values.

Python has a built-in function bool () that can be used to transform any value to a Boolean and check if the value can be interpreted as true or false.

Let's see an example:

odd_numbers = (1, 2, 3, 4, 5, 6)

x = 2 in odd numbers

x

false

y = 4 in even_numbers

y = true

If an element has a "none value", it means that it lacks a precise value.

9. Conversions

Python has some built-in function that allow you to convert elements. Here you can see how:

tuple(l) → to convert a list to a tuple

list(t) → to convert a tuple to a list

CHAPTER ELEVEN: SYNTAX

We have just gotten in touch with the various types of data in Python. Now, we should find out which commands can be used.

First, we will look into the indentation; second, we will explain the control flow statements – if, for, while, break, continue, and pass.

<u>Indentation</u>

The indentation is one of the most characterizing syntactic elements of Python.

Let's see a classic example:

```
def perm(l):
    # Compute the list of all permutations of l
    if len(l) <= 1:
         return [l]
    r = []
    for i in range(len(l)):
```

```
        s = l[:i] + l[i+1:]
        p = perm(s)
        for x in p:
            r.append(l[i:i+1] + x)
    return r
```

As you can see, it is easy to see where the code ends and where the following code line starts.

The indentation is used to indicate a block of code. Obviously you must indent each block with the same amount of spaces. In Python, we use indentations to indicate to what block a particular string of code belongs.

Another great feature is that the universal block closing rules are universal, so we do not need to specify *end, endif, fi,* parentheses or brackets, *wend, endwhile, next, loop, end procedure or end function.* We only need to respect the *indentation*.

The IF statement

What is a *Control Flow Statement*? It's a feature that allows the program to take decisions, depending on the situation, reading the code in a particular order. We can control the statement execution using some control flow tools.

The IF instruction is probably the most used command among all programming languages.

We can use IF to check a condition.

Here is an example of how IF works:

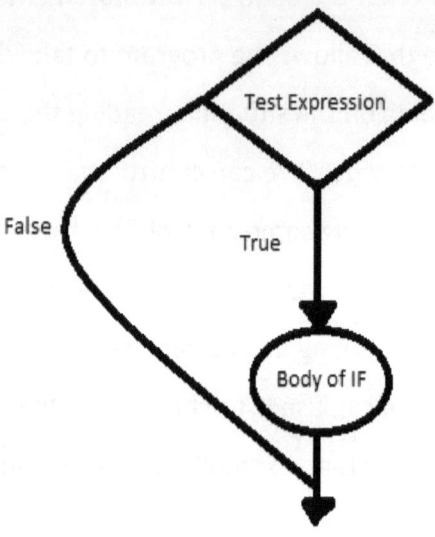

We run a block of statement only if the condition IF is true; otherwise, we operate another statement.

Example of IF statement syntax:

x = int(input("Please enter an integer: "))
Please enter an integer: 42

```
if x < 0:
x = 0
print('Negative changed to zero')
 elif x == 0:
print('Zero')
elif x == 1:
print ('Single')
 else:
print('more')
```

More

We can observe ":" that we used to end the test that controls the program flow.

You can insert as many *Elif as* you need; in the example above, the last Elif is not obligatory.

The FOR statement

The For instruction allows us to define iterations. To decide how many iterations we need and on which element we have to perform the iteration, we must use any object we can consider sequence.

Traditionally used to repeat a string of code an exact number of times.

We have already seen many sequence examples: lists, tuple, strings. These are all data we can use to iterate with For:

for c in "abc":

Print c

A

B

C

>>>

How can we execute a simple iteration a certain number of times without having the right sequence?

We could use "range"

for n range (4):
Print n
1
2
3
4
>>>

*With the command "range", we can also choose the start and the end of an iteration.

"For" allows us also to execute a cycle on more variables at the same time.

This is possible due to the fact that the "items" method in a dictionary gives a list of *tuples* composed by their own key and value.

"For" establishes a cycle on every element in this list and gives to the variables *key* and *value* the values we have in each *tuple*.

The WHILE statement

The *While* instruction is similar to the *For* instruction. The only difference is that the iteration is not based on a fixed sequence but executes the operation as long as the given condition is true.

Here is an example of how While works:

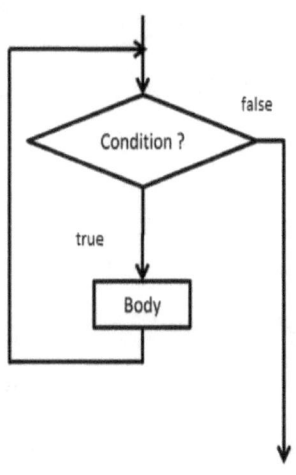

x = 1

while x < 7:

Print x

X += 1

1

2

3

4

5

6

>>>

In the example above, (the increment statement), is executed until the count remains below 7.

If a condition remains True, we have a so-called "Infinite Loop". In that case, you should press CTRL + C to close the program.

<u>The Break and Continue</u>

Break and Continue are used to stop an iteration to pass to the next one.

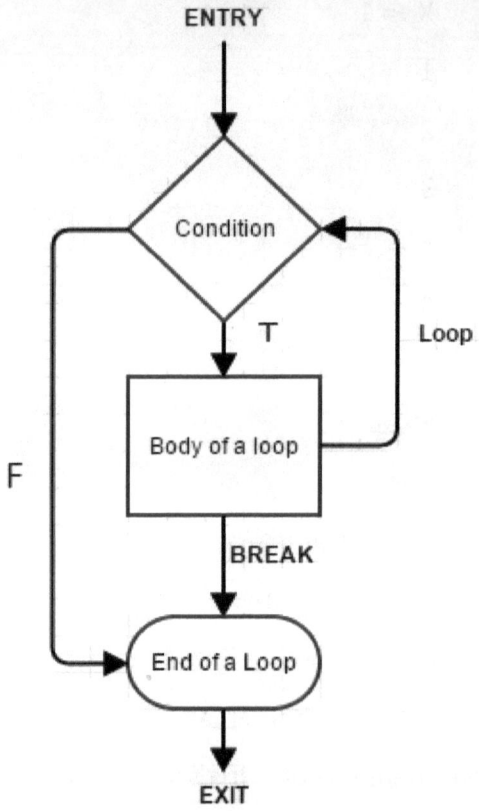

You will often use *Break* in *for loop* and *while loop* as in these classic examples:

For var in sequence:

 # codes inside for loop

If condition:

   Break

 # codes inside for loop

#codes outside for loop

While test expression:

 # codes inside while loop

If condition:

   Break

 # codes inside the loop

 # codes outside while loop

Now that we have gotten in touch with the instructions *break* and *continue,* let's step back to *for* and *while* because they have another peculiarity, the instruction: *Else.*

It was an *If* clause, but *"else"* is also very useful with cycles due to the fact that all the instructions we will write in *else* will be executed at the cycle end (if we do not end the cycle first with a *break*).

Example of if – else

Num = 8

If num >= 5:
Print("positive or zero")
Else
Print("negative number")

*try with different numbers as well

With this program, you can check if the number is positive, negative, or zero.

CHAPTER TWELVE: FUNCTIONS

What is a function?

It is a block of code used to perform a specific task.

Through *Functions,* we can break our program. This allows us to have better modularity in favor of organization and better reusability.

We usually come across 3 different types of functions in Python:

1. User-Defined Functions; functions created by the user

2. Built-in Functions; (list below)

3. Anonymous Functions; also known as Lambda Functions, are created in Python using a construction called "lambda".

Here is a list of: Built-in Functions

➢ Python abs()	➢ *returns absolute value of a number*
➢ Python any()	➢ *Checks if any Element of an Iterable is True*
➢ Python all()	➢ *returns true when all elements in iterable is true*
➢ Python ascii()	➢ *Returns String Containing Printable Representation*
➢ Python bin()	➢ *converts integer to binary string*
➢ Python bool()	➢ *Coverts a Value to Boolean*
➢ Python bytearray()	➢ *returns array of given byte size*
➢ Python	➢ *Checks if the Object is*

callable()	*Callable*
➢ Python bytes()	➢ *returns immutable bytes object*
➢ Python chr()	➢ *Returns a Character (a string) from an Integer*
➢ Python compile()	➢ *Returns a Python code object*
➢ Python classmethod()	➢ *returns class method for given function*
➢ Python complex()	➢ *Creates a Complex Number*
➢ Python delattr()	➢ *Deletes Attribute from the Object*
➢ Python dict()	➢ *Creates a Dictionary*
➢ Python dir()	➢ *Tries to Return Attributes of Object*
➢ Python divmod()	➢ *Returns a Tuple of*

	Quotient and Remainder
➤ Python enumerate()	➤ *Returns an Enumerate Object*
➤ Python staticmethod()	➤ *creates static method from a function*
➤ Python filter()	➤ *constructs iterator from elements which are true*
➤ Python eval()	➤ *Runs Python Code Within Program*
➤ Python float()	➤ *returns floating point number from number, string*
➤ Python format()	➤ *returns formatted representation of a value*

- Python frozenset()
  - Python getattr()
  - Python globals()
  - Python exec()
  - Python hasattr()
  - Python help()
  - Python hex()
  - Python hash()
  - Python input()
  - Python

- *returns immutable frozenset object*
  - *returns value of named attribute of an object*
  - *returns dictionary of current global symbol table*
  - *Executes Dynamically Created Program*
  - *returns whether object has named attribute*
  - *Invokes the built-in Help System*
  - *Converts to Integer to Hexadecimal*
  - *returns hash value of an object*
  - *reads and returns a line of string*
  - *Returns Identify of an*

id()	Object
➢ Python isinstance()	➢ *Checks if a Object is an Instance of Class*
➢ Python int()	➢ *returns integer from a numberor strings*
➢ Python issubclass()	➢ *Checks if a Object is Subclass of a Class*
➢ Python iter()	➢ *returns iterator for an object*
➢ Python list() Function	➢ *creates list in Python*
➢ Python locals()	➢ *returns dictionary of current local symbol table*
➢ Python len()	➢ *Returns Length of an Object*

- Python max()
- returns largest element

- Python min()
- returns smallest element

- Python map()
- Applies Function and Returns a List

- Python next()
- Retrieves Next Element from Iterator

- Python memoryview()
- returns memory view of an argument

- Python object()
- Creates a Featureless Object

- Python oct()
- converts integer to octal

➢ Python ord()	➢ *returns Unicode code point for Unicode character*
➢ Python open()	➢ *Returns a File object*
➢ Python pow()	➢ *returns x to the power of y*
➢ Python print()	➢ *Prints the Given Object*
➢ Python property()	➢ *returns a property attribute*
➢ Python range()	➢ *return sequence of integers between start and stop*
➢ Python	➢ *returns printable*

repr()	*representation of an object*
➢ Python reversed()	➢ *returns reversed iterator of a sequence*
➢ Python round()	➢ *rounds a floating point number to ndigits places.*
➢ Python set()	➢ *returns a Python set*
➢ Python setattr()	➢ *sets value of an attribute of object*
➢ Python slice()	➢ *creates a slice object specified by range()*
➢ Python sorted()	➢ *returns sorted list from a given iterable*
➢ Python str()	➢ *returns informal representation of an object*

➢ Python sum()	➢ *Add items of an Iterable*
➢ Python tuple() Function	➢ *Creates a Tuple*
➢ Python type()	➢ *Returns Type of an Object*
➢ Python vars()	➢ *Returns __dict__ attribute of a class*
➢ Python zip()	➢ *Returns an Iterator of Tuples*
➢ Python __import__()	➢ *Advanced Function Called by import*
➢ Python super()	➢ *Allow you to Refer Parent Class by super*

The instruction that allows us to create a function is *Def*.

Example:

Def fact (n):

    If n < 2:

Return 1

    Return n * fact (n – 1)

The function *Fact* accepts only one parameter, named "n". The *return* instruction is used to end the function giving back the right number.

As you can see in the last example, we can find:

- The keyword *def* followed by the function name
- An argument (n)
- To mark the end of the function, we use a colon (:)

- With the same indentation level, we write another valid statement to create the function body.
- A final *return* statement to exit the function.

```
Def functionname( parameters ):
    "function_docstring"
Function_suite
    Return [expression]
```

Docstring: A *docstring* is used to explain what that function does. It is optional, but sometimes, you need to document what you're writing.

Return: The *return* statement is used to exit a function and hand back a value to its caller.

How do functions work in Python?

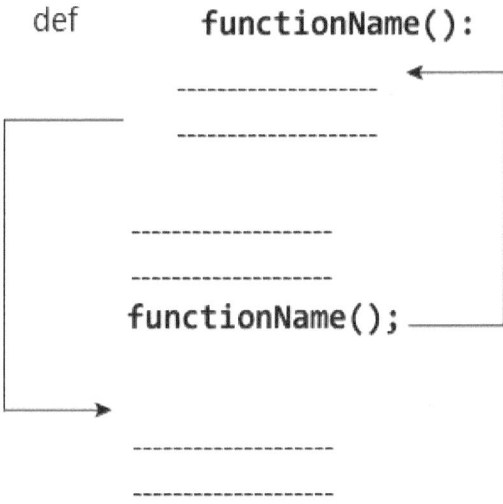

With a function, you can:

- Define the function
- Call a function

How to define a function

You can easily define a function using the keywords *def*, as previously shown, to declare a function. Subsequently, the programmer will add parameters (within parenthesis) to the function as well as statements to be executed to the function itself. At the end, insert the *return* statement to exit the function.

Call a function

What "calling a function means"

Calling a function is the process to execute the function you have defined. You can call a function either from the Python prompt or through other functions.

The return Statement

In the previous section, you have already seen the *return* statement. Basically, it gives something back or replies to the function caller (*print command* only produces text*).*

When a function ends without the *return* statement, it is the same as a *return None*.

All the below functions [F1, F2, F3] will give back a *None:*

```
def f1():
    pass
def f2():
    return
def f3():
    return None
```

We can also verify it in *IDLE:*

```
>>> print  f1(),  f2(),  f3()
None  None  None
>>>
```

CHAPTER THIRTEEN: CLASSES

Now that we've seen the types of data, syntax, and functions, we are going to merge them to learn to create new classes in Python.

First, we should define what a class is as well as what an object is:

An object is an encapsulation of variables and functions into a single entity. A class is a template that you can use to create objects.

The Classes provide objects with valiables and functions.

We can say that a class is a blueprint to create objects.

So, let's jump into that by creating our first class! First, we have to define a class with the *class operator*:

# Defining a class
class class_name:

[statement 1]

[statement 2]

[statement 3]

[etc.]

Now, we've created a new local namespace where we can define the attributes of the given class; attributes are data or functions.

We can access data and functions through the class objects that were authomatically created when we created our class.

In order to access attributes and to add new objects of a class, we have to use this class object.

Finally, we can create an object. The procedure is straight forward as usual:

ob = MyClass()

We just created a new instance object that we named ob.

Objects and attributes can be easily deleted using the del statement. Let's see an example:

c1 = ComplexNumber(1,3)

del c1

c1

Classes include methods. A method is basically a function that takes a class instance as its first parameter.

Let's make an example:

class movies:

"sub categories of movies"

def _init_(self, horror=0 ,

thriller=0 ,

drama=0) :

self.horror = horror

self.thriller = thriller

self.drama = drama

CHAPTER FOURTEEN: **WHAT CAUSES FATAL ERRORS AND HOW TO FIX IT**

If you encounter fatal exception errors whenever you use your PC, then you are probably wondering why it happens and what causes them. Basically, the fatal exception is an error message that many PC users encounter as they use their computers. This particular error will indicate that the program you are running and the one that caused the error will need to be closed.

The fatal exception error simply means the exception cannot be handled in order for the program to continue running.

You have to understand that software programs need to communicate with the operating system through layers of codes. When the operating system encounters an invalid code or an illegal software program instruction, it will usually result in the fatal exception error.

Generally, fatal exception errors are caused by incompatibility of the programs you try running. It can also be caused by improperly written programs, as well as hardware related issues, such as overheating of a specific hardware.

There are quite a lot of causes for fatal exception errors. So, here are some effective solutions that may solve this problem.

The first is by disabling any programs running that may cause a conflict between the programs that are already running and the programs that you try running. By disabling a particular program first, you will be able to prevent fatal exception errors.

You might also want to delete temporary files, as this is also a common cause for fatal exception errors.

Defragmenting the hard drive as well as running Scandisk will prevent data corruption, which is also a cause of fatal exception errors.

CHAPTER FIFTHEEN: BEST PRACTICES FOR HANDLING WEBSITE ERRORS

This chapter explains the process of implementing error handling for a website that utilizes server-side scripting. Proper error handling is necessary to ensure that users of a website have a good experience during their visit. Any professional website should be thoroughly tested on a staging server before being deployed on the live web server. However, it is not always possible to anticipate every possible error, and good error handling will notify both the user and the webmaster about problems with the website in a production environment.

When we talk about website errors, there are two different types we need to talk about. Fatal errors cause execution of the script to halt and a page error (HTTP status code 501) to be reported to the user. An exception is an error thrown by a server-side script that may be captured through scripting and allow the web page to be displayed. An example of this kind of exception is a database query, which causes an exception but doesn't abort execution of the current script.

Building a Code Library

In order to provide consistent error handling throughout a website, a shared code module should be created that provides the majority of the error handling details. The goal here is not to repeat code so that everything is handled in one central location. That way, any changes or modifications that need to be made to the code only have to be done once. A good error handling library will contain methods for displaying a friendly message to the visitor and collecting all the debugging information needed for technical support.

Every programming language is different, so it will be up to the developer to decide how to implement the error handling. The goal should be to make it flexible and intuitive, so it can be used in many different scenarios. It should only require a minimal amount of code to wrap a section of scripting code with error handling.

Displaying Friendly Messages

There are various options for displaying friendly error messages to the user. One option is to stop processing of the entire page and display an error that reads "Sorry, this web page cannot be displayed at this time due to an internal issue. Our technical support team has been notified and will work quickly to resolve this issue." This is often the best way to handle any unexpected errors that we can handle through server-side scripting.

Another option is to display as much of the page as possible and place a highly visible error message on the screen. This message would read "Unable to perform the action due to an internal error." The point of this type of handling is that we give the user the opportunity to correct the issue and attempt the action again. This type of situation is typically a form submission where bad data causes an error on the web page.

Debug Information

When the server-side code can handle the error, it is important that debug information is sent to the webmaster and technical support team, so issues can be resolved quickly. This debug information is different from the friendly error message displayed to the user. It contains detailed information about the code that caused the error and any other pertinent information.

One of the most common errors is a database error due to a malformed SQL statement for websites that do not use stored procedures. This type of error can easily be caught and handled through server-side code. In this case, the type of debug information we would like to see is the source of the error (file name and line number) with a stack trace and the offending SQL script that caused the error.

Some other bits of information we would like to see is the URL including the query string. The request method (GET or POST) and all form variables are passed to the script. Additionally, any cookies set on the client's machine would also be beneficial to reproduce the error. The point is, we need to get as much information as possible, so the issue can be identified and corrected quickly.

Transmitting Debug Information

Once we have this debug information, we need to transmit it to the webmaster and tech support team. The easiest way of doing this is to send an e-mail containing all the above information. Another method is to store this information in a database accessible through a company intranet.

You should consider doing both to eliminate the possibility that one method fails. Of course, if the whole script fails and stops executing, then no information will be sent out. This is one of the dangers of error handling. As a precaution to avoid this, website owners should periodically test their error handling to make sure everything works.

Webmaster Alerts

As mentioned, notifications about errors can be delivered via emai. Sometimes, it doesn't make sense to have your inbox filled with lots of e-mails. An alternative is to create an RSS Feed. RSS stands for Really Simple Syndication or Rich Site Summary. It is like a news feed that delivers headlines along with a synopsis to users.

Using an RSS reader application, users can receive notifications through their computer or cell phone about new error reports that get generated. There are lots of code libraries available for creating RSS services on a website. It is also not too difficult to create your own custom service since an RSS feed is not much more than a dynamically-generated XML document that conforms to the RSS specification.

For even faster response times, it is fairly trivial to add a notification (or alert system) using SMS or text messaging to a cell phone number. So just like a pager was used long ago, site owners will be notified instantly whenever an issue occurs. Since it is a text message, information such as the page URL or error type can also be sent in the alert.

CHAPTER SIXTEEN: WHY PYTHON IS HERE TO STAY

Python was originally conceived by Van Rossum as a hobby language in December 1989. Also, the major and backward-incompatible version of the general-purpose programming language was released on December 3, 2008. But Python has been recently rated by a number of surveyors as the most popular coding language of 2015. The massive popularity indicates Python's effectiveness as a modern programming language. At the same time, Python 3 is currently used by developers across the world for creating a variety of desktop GUI, web, and mobile applications. There are also a number of reasons the huge popularity and market share of Python will remain intact over a longer period of time.

8 Reasons the Massive Popularity of Python Will Remain Intact in the Future

1) Supports Multiple Programming Paradigms

Good developers often take advantage of different programming paradigms to reduce the amount of time and effort required for developing large and complex applications. Like other modern programming languages, Python supports a number of commonly used programming styles, including object-oriented, functional, procedural, and imperative. It further features automatic memory management, along with a dynamic type system. So programmers can use the language to effectuate development of large and complex software applications.

2) Doesn't Require Programmers to Write Lengthy Code

Python is designed with a complete focus on code readability. So the programmers can create a readable code base that can be used by members of distributed teams. At the same time, the simple syntax of the programming language enables them to express concepts without writing long lines of code. The feature makes it easier for developers to work on large and complex applications. As they can easily skip certain tasks required by other programming languages, it becomes easier for developers to maintain and update their applications.

3) Provides a Comprehensive Standard Library

Python further scores over other programming languages due to its extensive standard library. The programmers can use these libraries to accomplish a variety of tasks without writing long lines of code. Also, the standard library of Python is designed with a large number of high use programming tasks scripted into it. Thus, it helps programmers to accomplish tasks like string operations, development, and implementation of web services, working with internet protocols and handling operating system interface.

4) Effectuates Web Application Development

Python is designed as a general-purpose programming language and lacks built-in web development features. Web developers use a variety of add-on modules to write modern web applications in Python. While writing web applications in Python, programmers have the option to use several high-level web frameworks, including Django, web2py, TurboGears, CubicWeb, and Real. These web frameworks help programmers to perform a number of operations, without writing additional code, like database manipulation, URL routing, session storage and retrieval, and output template formatting. They can further use the web frameworks to protect the web application from cross-site scripting attacks, SQL injection, and cross-site request forgery.

5) Facilitates Development of High-Quality GUI, Scientific, and Numeric Applications

Python is currently available on major operating systems, like Windows, Mac OS X, Linux, and UNIX. So the desktop GUI applications written in the programming language can be deployed on multiple platforms. The programmers can further speed up cross-platform desktop GUI application development using frameworks like Kivy, wxPython, and PyGtk. A number of reports have highlighted that Python is used widely for the development of numeric and scientific applications. While writing scientific and numerical applications in Python, developers can take advantage of tools like Scipy, Pandas, IPython, along with the Python Imaging Library.

6) Simplifies Prototyping of Applications

Nowadays, each organization wants to beat the competition by developing software with distinct and innovative features. That is why prototyping has become an integral part of the modern software development lifecycle. Before writing the code, developers have to create a prototype of the application to display its features and functionality to various stakeholders. As a simple and fast programming language, Python enables programmers to develop the final system without putting any extra time and effort. At the same time, developers also have the option to start developing the system straight from the prototype simply by refactoring the code.

7) Can also be used for Mobile App Development

Frameworks like Kivy also make Python usable for developing mobile apps. As a library, Kivy can be used for creating both desktop applications and mobile apps. But it allows developers to write the code once and deploy the same code on multiple platforms. Along with interfacing with the hardware of the mobile device, Kivy comes with built-in camera adapters, modules to render and play videos, and modules to accept user input through multi-touch and gestures. Thus, programmers can use Kivy to create different versions of the same applications for iOS, Android, and Windows Phones. Also, the framework does not require developers to write long lines of code while creating Kivy programs. After creating different versions of the mobile app, they can package the app separately for the individual app store. The option makes it easier for developers to create different versions of the mobile app without deploying separate developers.

8) Open Source

Despite being rated as the most popular coding language of 2015, Python is still available as open source and free software. Along with large IT companies, startups and freelance software developers can use the programming language without paying any fees or royalty. Thus, Python makes it easier for businesses to reduce development cost significantly. At the same time, programmers can avail the assistance from the large and active community to add out-of-box features to software applications.

CONCLUSION

Python is a strong programming language that provides easy use of the code lines, great maintenance handling, and easy debugging. It has gained importance across the globe as Google has made it one of its official programming languages.

Python is a popular choice among programmers due to its simple syntax and its ease in debugging and error fixing.

Similar to many other interpretative languages, Python offers more flexibility than compiled languages, and it can be efficiently used to integrate disparate systems. Certainly, Python is a versatile programming language with several applications used in diverse fields.

Now that you have reached the end of this book, you should be able to comprehend the basics of Python and write simple lines of codes. You should also be able to comprehend the difference between the various types of data, the syntax in Python, the most important functions and modules. Although the road to become a successful programmer is still long, I hope this book will pave the path for your success, and I'm positive that, if you use the knowledge contained in it in the right way, it will definitely help you reach your goals.

Thanks for reaching the end of this book, and I hope you enjoyed it.

www.ingramcontent.com/pod-product-compliance
Lightning Source LLC
Chambersburg PA
CBHW030656220526
45463CB00005B/1797